# Goodbyes Are Hellos

*Poems by*
*Michael Torok*

Goodbyes Are Hellos

Copyright © 2015 by Michael Torok

Cover art by Joshua J. Hunt

Author photo by Karen Wolcott

All rights reserved. Printed in the United States of America. No part of this book may be reproduced or transmitted in any form or by any means without written permission.

ISBN 978-0-9963030-0-2

Published by Smokeloop Press

## Acknowledgements:

Grateful acknowledgement is given to those publications in which many of these poems first appeared:

*Clackamas Literary Review*
*Fox Cry Review*
*Louisiana Review*
*Northridge Review*
*Red Rock Review*
*The Refined Savage*
*The Smoking Poet*

*For Karen,*
*who has always inspired and encouraged me,*
*and my son Jack,*
*who has taught me more than he might ever realize.*

**Goodbyes are Hellos**

## Horizontal Accretion

Louisiana's moon imposes herself
at the end of the road —
large enough to swallow the truck
if he could reach her
in time. Racing desperately,
the bruise of sunset
behind him, to break the skin
and be enveloped in the warm milk
of craters and dust. Comfortable and constant,
two things his whitening knuckles,
complete in their own betrayals,
hold before and away from him, she rises. Silence,
his only bounty, as she steadily climbs
higher and farther away. He stops.
Waiting to begin again
the chase east, knowing he must
catch her before the ocean
consumes them both.

Remembering ...

the surrender you offered.
Small whispers of wind cycloning
dust at my feet
planted by the willow.

We were young. Making snow
angels in my parents' yard
after midnight. Your hair
in my face, pushing down
on my pelvis with all your weight —
to make the impressions deeper.

Salt-drenched in the dark,
in the backseat,
I listened
to the springs, concentrating
on sustaining, drinking
the smell of our sweat.

You kept me away the night
your brother met a pole
in our car. We shared everything
but you.

You bled away innocence for me.
He shut down the rural route.

Tapping the reserves now,
buried deep in our yard impressions,
knowing I can never
pull your blood from the soil,
give it back,
silently trying.

## Wombsong

I tried to please you. Done so,
so long, I couldn't remember
my name only attach it
to you. Sleeping, tired as the wind
must get touching waves, back
arching and falling— cresting
the mind, dropping to gutter.
Shoving my head into you,
I wanted to come home — carry you
to the grave, as mother — wanted
to replace one noose for another.
You closed your legs hard
on my ears. I could hear
the ocean of your insides waiting
for my baptism, could smell the salt
of desire. You laughed as my teeth circled
the inside of thigh. We fell
to shore together, my tears mixing
with the sounds of desire.
Tomorrow you will be able to count
my adult teeth, one by one.

Fair Trade

Sudden bursts no longer come
when I close my eyes. Silver does
not grace the black velvet jacket, worn
in Texas July. It no longer graces every
digit, but sleeps in the veins
of my hair and shatters down
my back, dormant, as we watch the band,
swaying instead of dancing.

I remember silver, a topic
of conversation at one of the salons. Silver
in my poetry, a draw, a repetition,
a girl I wanted. I remember lying,
making up meaning for color, standing self-
reflexive and leaving with
whom I came. That night, I first saw
the silver, abundant.

My son, the last time I saw real
silver, when he was born, reaching, bluing, torn
between the one who shed him
and the beautiful wrinkled nut of flesh.
The orderly pulling me aside, after the scale,
asking me to follow. Leaving, rounding
the corner to watch them pound
and pound on him. The shock and glint
of stethoscopes as they forced him
to expel the dormancy, clinging
to the rails, shaking to let go
of her.

Treasure

At the age of twenty-five
he carried with him
three shells at all times.
They kept a rhythm
when he walked against
his left breast. Sometimes
he'd show them to close
friends — always shocked
by the first one.
                A tin
Christ, sans cross and arms,
crucified all the same,
about five inches high
he'd lay carefully face
up on a table. He'd never
show without proper space,
a table – preferably carved
with initials.
                When Christ
was dead center, he'd pull
the second from his pocket.
A wedding band, highly polished,
bright shining, cresting the tin
head. He'd balance it,
like a nickel on edge,
and make sure the shadow
cut under Christ's chin.
Then, and only when
it was right — a
rarity, he'd reveal the
third.

                    Slipped
from a dimestore star
scroll tube, a rolled photo
torn in half, only
the white back showing,
he'd arrange as arms.
Straight out, ragged edges
toward the broken torso.

Weightless

I will not forget the woman
I pushed off the bench with my kiss
in front of friends,
catching her head before we hit
filthy tile, the full impact
caught in my hand.

My bruised knuckles on the steering wheel
a reminder the next day
of spent passion,
an end before lost beginnings,
a physical need I have
kept silent:
no accident
no whimsy
no mistake.

The need to fall.

The Dream

He had three recurring dreams,
since childhood, folded neatly
at the foot of the bed.
The first of astronauts
he had launched too soon
into space — unable to hold back
an eager finger-
on-button reflex guilt.
In the seconds after
Lift-off, he would wake
howling.

He could feel the second coming
in the half conscious
before images became solid
dream — an apprehensive, disembodied
presence. A hallway,
never-ending, stretched before
him. Curved up at the sides,
the sewers of childhood
games played. Large shapes,
round and oval, swept
up and down and over
the walls and floors waiting
to crush his oncoming
body. Behind him, the presence
formed in half-sleep
chased him — able to pass
through obstructions unharmed.
He'd always wake when
a round shape

had already crushed his legs
and pelvis, ribs punctured lungs
and heart — his last awareness,
the heavy smoothness coming
for his head.

The last was of a blonde
haired girl, glowing in
the headlights of his beaten
black Oldsmobile. She stood in
the rain-slick road twirling
and twirling — a child's
game of *fall down* and he could not
stop. The brake pedal fell flaccid
to the floor under his foot.
The steering locked, but she never stopped
twirling until he saw the fragile face
of his daughter crack the windshield
with a mixture of blood,
glass, night, and rain.

This final dream will not recur,
it has left him.
As his wife enters the women's clinic
before him, he knows that what it foretold,
he has brought to harvest.

Biodegradable Memoriam

Clutching an airmailed note
in an ironic grin, he climbs
bridge tiers.

Cresting the edge of fiction,
his toes grip tight girders
spread web-like over the Bay,
teetering then swaying in high wind.
Touching clouds above the highway,
releasing the city below,
hiding in billows the memory
of company gone for good —
or just forever.

Pulling back from the cloud break
to the 3x3 cement safety-island tower,
lying down, legs dangling free in understanding—
the ease of inching
off, not having to look both ways,

backward nor forward.

The Selling of Joseph
   — *after Samuel Sewall*

When I met him, he could
not remember exactly how
the gun had come to discharge.
The felicity of the moment —
snapped as trace powder filtered
through stagnant sunlight to settle
on his shaking, well-calloused hand —
almost invisible on ashen skin.
He did not try to run, then,
but waited for the police to take
him. Knew the neighbors called.

When I met him, he blamed
the drugs he had taken, not
the inconstancy of his wife, not
the Corinthian motivations of his best
friend, not yet himself — only abstraction,
rage. He must have sensed my fear,
after he told me, and felt for me.
I was, then, a visiting writer to his cellblock,
encouraging journals and letters
of apology. He liked me, my stories, wanted
to try, could not write.

When I met him, I found myself,
a stenographer. *I wanna say I'm sorry*
*for shooting my wife. I shouldn'ta*
*done that.* I stopped writing,
his candor the clearest sign.

## Lost Saturday (*Decree Nisi Secundus*)

When the body rebels, leaving you
to answer your son at 7am, without
good morning, only a bleary-eyed
grunt followed by heavy yellow coughing,
with the knowledge that no one
is coming, no one is going to appear,
Copperfield-like, to offer a set of eyes,
comforting hands, warm tea. It is now
that you realize what it means.
       The TV
glow you would normally want to extinguish,
the knowledge that, even if you swallowed
your pride, picked up the phone, asked
his mother for help, she would not be there.
Infection's cloying smell drifting down your
throat.
  You know now, every bit of you
wanting to curl in a ball, ride the black
crashing waves into shore, be battered,
sucked back out into the seas of slumber, darkly
wanting him to just go away — leave you
to illness.
      Yes, now you know.

Disintegration

Sleep fog thick in my eyes
after driving all night,
burning away as we spar, even
now.

    You have been waiting.
The ceramic tile of the kitchen
floor unyielding, angry as heat pours
from the stove, on and forgotten,
dispersing the sanitized cool of the air
conditioner.

           One ear listens to you,
the other to our son's sleep,
fretful and haunted in his room, the monsters
only feet away. Failing
to keep their voices down.

What It Means to Pray

Tonight I realized,
father, that it is you
I pray to, whose name is not
Yahweh, but Brut
by Faberge, on a good night.
Blessed soft-chinned kisses
before bedtime. Bad nights,
sand paper cheeks or the strop.

Treading the water in my drink,
your eyes still clear in the picture
that watches me,
taken long before I knew to add ice
to the Ouzo or understood clouds
as cataracts or the frustration
of shaking hands.

The Baker's Sheepdogs

I.
No, it was not just
one but many — three should
truth become an option.
Molly was old, a veteran
chaser of mobility — cars,
trucks, children. Everyone knew
to watch out for her, growling
as Father or Mother pulled
into the street. She would wait
until the target, prey, was halfway
down the street
before tearing chunks of grass
in her initial lunge. Rarely,
she would beat the car
to the stop sign, not the point.
She knew cars stop, dogs
don't have to. Smart.
Bark, bite, never hold
on, bumpers safer
than tires — a sport.
Motorcycles have spokes, no
bumper, wheel, and Molly
won. A new driver,
going too slow, still
in second gear. Fast enough
to catch a paw, broken,
followed by teeth, broken
neck. Children gathered to pay
respect. The driver was fine.

II.
Bar was young, stupid, male,
impulsive. He did not know
the rules, the game. One blue
eye never focused with the brown,
the first sheepdog that hair
did not blind. Bar
got a fence he outgrew. Again,
pulling into the street
was roulette. The tiles
blue or brown instead of red
or black. If the car focused,
the fence disappeared — cleared
without a problem. He caught
cars halfway, ran along
side, sometimes for blocks.
It was a semi, momentarily
out of focus, and so much air
between wheels on the trailer.
Bar went for the crossover
and lost. The rear end
caught up, but the driver
never stopped.

III.
*Sabatchka* never had a name.
She was sure to be
a Molly junior, a second.
So much front yard green
to snap dragonflies, paw-
landed beetles, catch the rare
turtle. Tiny claws, teeth
too young to break
skin, a community dog
from the start. The children's
dog, but Jim — the token owner —
had a brother who kept
him busy the day neighbors
moved in. *Sabatchka* did
not know there was a game.
Molly and Bar knew that
moving vans were easy,
they always stop, not prey.
*Sabatchka* saw opportunity
only. Caught it, first
time out.

Columbia Road Beach, Lake Erie:
    an explanation of sorts

Remember the stairs
ending at the water —
a sweating six-pack
waiting at the butt
of each iron railing.

We'd strip off
teenage anger and fear,
leave our modesty on the steps
and meet the lake,
bare.

Nibbling fish,
easy laughter among friends,
sudden bravado. Accidental hands
touching under green
waves.

The boys would never come
out onto the steps, ashamed
but happy in the knowledge
of water and the excuse
of women.

Options Other than the Back

I am frustrated with my body
pushing in certain areas to feel
the yield of skin and hope
that whatever is displaced
will stay where pushed. Sometimes
it seems to want to, while
more often the back flow
is immediate and more derisive —
having borne witness to the possible,
the alternative present comes harder
than before. It does not stop
with the relocation of muscle
mass and fatty tissue – the pressure
-induced plastic surgery —
but takes on the air of daydream,
a waking nightmare of wasted space.
The desire to see the entire skin
surface at one time, ignoring
any other function it may have outside
the aesthetic, to have it all
face front, a type of size camouflage,
an intimidation technique — the cobra's
head, or a mating aid shed
like peacock feathers after success.
To be able to flare
and contract this hidden excess
like great leather wings,
possibly pleated or folded
when not in use, draping
at my sides, always viable,
able to be accosted at all times

by more than one of the senses —
without the deception of mirrors.
A constant need to know
that half of me has not disappeared.

Moth Wings

With eyes curious and intent
I waited while the old
man, careful as his age, turned
the leaf to allow a child,
me, to see velvet wings asleep. Closed,
they were larger than my
hand spread to capture,
the texture and form of knotted wood
painted in fairy dust —
too fragile to sustain the dumb fingers
of youth reaching and smearing
perfectly outlined wood grains
to a mud brown. Too late,
the old man explained,
as he gave the once regal night
insect, now enclosed in a jar,
to me, the importance of beauty
I could not touch.

Bean

We killed her, you
and I, a perfect nut,
a delicate first tendril grasp
cut. And I complied, as did you,

much more capable
then, without the knowledge
of what it meant to have
him.

Our second child, the one
we decided to allow.
The child who showed us
exactly how little we had, together.

A smile in our bed
we alone could not sustain.
We left one another, abandoned
fallow ground, the promise,

for empty earth, a null harvest,
understanding seasons late what was
left without
her.

Sistine

I saw you today through stained glass eyes.
Hues shifting as I moved, then you.
A dance of blue and red,
the yellows rich,
eyes  kaleidoscoping
as I looked to you
for guidance

you offered me
a puzzle
of color.

Burrowing

He always took note
of the rabbits, the quiet
industry, the wariness of cats,
the garden's nibbled leaves.
They had made long tunnels
along the compost pile
throughout the backyard.
When younger, they were his
crusade. He would save them
from the tabby next door
careful to unload rocks
at the chaser, never hit
the chased. White tails
tearing around the house
to the safety of the back.

By the time he was mowing-
age, he knew to take care —
the power of the blade. Swift
turns did not allow time
for toads and moles to escape.
Lessons learned with the punctuation
of a heavy stone dropped
in mercy on the wounded.

Sensing danger from the new
machine, a mother began
digging a shallow in the front yard,
chancing the tabby's hunger
over the mower. Father
filled it in, the hole,
to smooth the lawn, discourage
the anomaly. The doe,
persistent, dug out the rocks
and dirt, smoothed rough walls,
and returned. Over and over,
cover and uncover, destroy
and mend, until she was tired.
Disappeared. And it was safe.

He paced the lawn,
oil and gas smoke chugging
from the mower in front
of him. It had been days
since he had seen the doe.
The hole was packed in,
untouched. He had checked.
He thought nothing as the blade
slowed and the engine strained. Clay
and dirt are tougher than grass.

Poesie

It is not the first time
I have screamed my poetry
into a corner
using its own voice.
Though, the last time,
it left me for five years,
dry, blowing with the dust,
my veins exposed
and brittle to touch.

Last night, I saw
the subtle shift, the eyeing of the door,
feet pointed one way,
body the other. I have grown
accustomed to checking body language,
her voice and tongue
practiced at revealing
nothing.

My exhaustion did not allow for speed.
Instead, I drank,
wetting my throat for the scream.

Cars
*— for father*

America was installed in me,
like a muffler system
or timing belt
in an Oldsmobile.

I held the light,
made sure the filter fit right;
three-quarter turn,
don't strip the thread.

Your hand always broke
free, circled mine on the light,
while the other steady-squeezed
the breather hose.

## Gloaming

He could taste the blue
stain on her tongue, hours
after she had finished
painting, a portrait of sorts,
on twisted sheets. Her body
first dipped and splattered
in latex and acrylic—
a blur of color drooled
meticulously—before embracing
the second canvas, one part
removed, to consummate
in final ferocity the sound
of red made visceral
through pigmented torsos.

Slipping Away from Me

I realize now that I lost my chance,
again, to Romeo. You have gone
first, as usual — I am
too cautious. The apothecary
letting me down, too squeamish
for the blade,
              a second time,
scars still healing, twenty years
later. The water in the tub
too cool — comfort not
found in the noise
of the faucet or the cold calm
of the blade.

A Prayer to Bartleby

And they did waste
you. With the frailty
of the anorexic, prostrate
to the wall-view they gave
you. A scribbler of others'
text until you could only prefer
not to. Possibility disappearing—
a dead letter office, art,
and you. An aesthetic
that swallows ability along
with probability. So, I come
to worship at the feet,
not punctured but curled –
protective. I come to inhabit
you, ball-fetal at the bottom
of wall-street's walled tombs.
And when I get inside, I will
ask you to prefer me,
your creation, to your creator.

Memory Tracks

He used to buy Jesus
from the garbage man at 34th
and the YMCA. He'd hide
behind the dumpster, slip his hand
pocket-side and slide holiness
out of silver-lined belief.
Wetting the spike of stigmata
for the last time
every day.

Porcelain

   —*for my very own Galatea*

You are tricky
when pushed, so often you do
not comply, but slump or fold.
Angry velvet under pressure.
I turn you on the wheel,
gloss and sweat mingling,
you have let me form you
tonight.

## Night Walk

I am laughing at myself in Texas, waltzing
country streets with my glass of wine
and my effeminate dog. She displays
down the street, showing coyotes
breeding.
    I take advantage of night
and country to walk in the pitch,
remembering a time when the rustle
of leaves meant investigate, instead
of run.
    She is perfect for me,
the dog, shying away from the darkest
areas, nearest the wooded tracts, forcing
me to act the hero, walk her through
my fear.

River Dreams

Walking broken china
in the kitchen, letting the pieces
make themselves known to my feet.
I remember buying it, china,
thinking of the Yangtze
the river people and their pottery.

Red stains on the linoleum
of the apartment and my eyes dry
as the carpet, now also stained
red with my footprints.
Little toes, but I can see the lines
in my feet.

Unlike when our son was born
and his skin was stretched
so tight across his preemie
body, so small you thought
he would blow out
of my convertible.

I shut the roof,
answering your worry with action,
thinking it was enough.
Finding, now, it never was. Sitting quietly
while I went to work everyday
estranged and beholden.

My son and my anger quietly
growing. Your desire
ebbing. I found you again, years
later, indifferent to my touch,
repulsed.

Sitting on the couch, pulling china from my feet.
I will spend hours pushing the blood
around the floor, not realizing
it is the only loss I can manage.

Soldier

The day I shot Mark
from across the backyard
with my BB gun, breaking
his favorite comb, seemingly safely
stashed in his back pocket,
I could not apologize
enough.

Inside, I was proud.
From the hip, I
sighted. Inside,
I was terrified
by the cool calculation. I
realized I could do something
horrible, easily, quickly,
detached from both ends
and means.
I became the perfect soldier
while vowing
never to be.

Last night, we fought,
and that same cool
slid into my stomach. Tendrils
of ice branching through
my chest.
I was again mercenary,
though, this time, provoked.

Nod — Delivery by Swallow

Against your back, I shake
like a junkie, my mouthed hallelujah caught
by your shoulder blades.
I travel the rosary of your spine,
Bumping my lips over you.

Your heart, under my fingers,
a moth careening against the porch
light. My eyes wet, catching the candle's
flame, as we drop together, wrapped
in tomorrow's pool of laundry.

My breathing slows
In your ear. Your heart regains
A steady tattoo as we settle
exhausted — black clouds skating
the moon —

New rhythms move us
into the night — my hand
in yours, the flowers fallen
from your hair, as I blur the stars,
our lids grown heavy.

## Hunting Dog

Our neighbor drives
up and over the drive and into
the lawn, pausing, idling before
the porch. It is eleven o'clock,
his dog has just groveled out
from under our house. Slipped
low into the darkness and weeds.
I greet him.
    *You seen that fuckin
dog?* I do not recognize
his anger, the dog is known
in our neighborhood, likes to visit
the other farms, get in
a bit of mischief. Last year
got pregnant by a Rottweiler.
She was a running joke, never
seen such a mixed up Beagle.
Smiling, I tell him where
she's gone. Shouldn't have.
                    *Gonna
kill that bitch.* Concerned, I give
a bit of a laugh, he doesn't.
He flicks on the truck's
dome light. From the vantage
of the porch, I see the hard blue-black
of his twelve gauge.

>                    *Killed four*
*a'my chickens tonight, seven hundred*
*bucks.* I can say nothing
as he asks me to hold her,
if I see her again. I nod, wave
as his lights burn our lawn white.
We walk inside as he cruises
slow down the street, searching,
the gun across his lap.
>                    I make
an excuse to bathe, run
the tub. Surrounded by cast
iron, I keep my head low,
fearing the shot. Under the water,
the tap booms, covers any unwanted
noise. I weigh the difference.

## He Spent the Afternoon without Me

I lit the night on fire
after you came home,
quietly. Tendrils of flame
licking at logs in the fireplace.
I wanted to do more
than cast a shadow across
the living room, sitting in the couch,
burning in the reflected light.

You took him, today,
to meet your lover. My blessing,
the agreement of an unredeemable,
granted. I saw him, running down
the street, returning to you
in the glare of sunlight, the eye
of imagination, vivid and unavoidable
now.

My son came home, speaking of cousins,
missing playmates, school, friends. His daughter,
your lover's, drew pictures — wooed him.
It was difficult to tell him no,
that it was time for bed,
that playtime was over.
Harder to tell him
than to tell you.

Geckos

Sleep fled the morning
I realized my mistake.
I left bed, left you, shook my head
at my son, asleep on the floor — he'd slipped
in during the night.

I slid open the porch door,
the south pulling my own humidity
to the surface, walking into the wake
of last night, inhaling us, salt,
sweat — little deaths.

I opened the water heater
closet and pulled the first sticky-trap
from the concrete slab. You
puffed at me, bright-eyed,
helplessly caught.

I wanted scorpions, centipedes…
never thought of you.

Waiting for the Bus

84 degrees at 6:54am and I
am waiting with my son
for the bus. I am not nostalgic
for my own bus rides, where
we waited pushing each other
and jockeying for social rank.
As early as second grade, places
and claims staked.

The rust belt provided dew
and 50s fathers, cool
even in August, and neighbor-
hood kids. My son waits
with me. When the bus comes,
he sneaks me a kiss on the cheek.
A simple solidarity.

A Last Cigarette

It wasn't about how much
we aimed at the moon,
it was the number of shots
we took at it. Never accepting
futility, only failure. Not recognizing
the beauty of the temples we'd built
as we continued to strive
for each defeat.
             Finally you told me
your love had died
three years previous. I had
not noticed.
       Smoke curling
forgotten around my fingers, caressing
the back of my hand, before the coal
left memories indelible.

Blur

And you with your needle eyes and mouth of fire
reminding me of empty alleys in which I
have awoken, shaking and cold,
trying to remember if the rust on my fingers
is mine or the reason my face hurts,
my arm, swollen and infected, my nose
leaking expenses onto my shirt.

The past you can invoke, though you were never
a part of it, no matter how much you wanted
to test the reality, see if I could take it,
you were never able,
until today, never capable of pulling the rage
through my skin — a prick, a subtle warmth, teased
into the dropper, burning.

Resolved Safely

Leaves collect in front of my door. I know
they invite nesting — earwigs bring scorpions, I'm told.
But, I like the crispness just before the decay takes hold,
moving from the bottom up.

Our son tracks the pest man's poison
into the house, granules the size of hourglass sand,
dropped from Spiderman tennies.
Spiders don't fair very well, either.

Though, yesterday, I found another centipede,
still fighting, seven inches of writhing black and red, near the cat bowl.
The boy never saw the trembling legs as I hit it with the dust brush.
Sweat beading on my lip as I tried to breathe,
calm the running cadence of my heart, the cramp of my fingers
around the pencil-thick brush handle.
Desperate to bolster weakened foundations,
the safety of home.

## Daddy

Think drunk, trying to make the world spin
so I can see it. Tired of believing. Need
to force myself to see to get back on my knees
to pray to a god that went away
a long time ago.
                You got me to do it sober,
easier liquor-breathed and high. Drinking
through my mouth-flood, my body's
attempt to save me.
                I've never let it.

Initial shivers climbing from my tail
into my scalp, bourbon burning, shaking
me as I swallow.
                It is the same feeling
as the first time I saw you;
as the way you walk toward me twenty-five
years later; as the smile you hide from me.

Throat-caught bile as our daughter
calls another man daddy. My son
no longer looks me in the eye.
                I need to drink
to stop the fear from freezing me. I need
the fear to make me feel.
I'd never dare be an alcoholic.
I am terrified of numb.

Return

Today, I went back to Houston,
my adopted dog and my son in the truck,
his cheek red-rimmed and swollen, the cut not
yet healed from unguarded teeth.

I did not need
to be told, "If he'd wanted to hurt
your son, he would've."
Though, I suppose, they felt
compelled.

I registered the shock of my admission,
"Yes, but I'm now afraid
of the dog." They were not ready
for confession.

I have always been able
to do so. This time, I simply volunteered
words to shut a door
I refused to leave
open.

Our dog stayed at the shelter,
"You let him fill a power vacuum,"
still lingering in the office as we left.

On the way home, three hours
of Texas highway in front of us,
my son's voice matched the rain
outside, "He is not
my best friend anymore?"

Oubliette

She is American now,
a little girl in a school full
of foreign sounds, a foundling, slightly
broken, palsied.

The lady who comes
to talk to her is not her mother, she
speaks in memory, asks the
easy questions: Мочу?
She offers no response,
no Да or нет, in kind.

She is silence,
a memory of gray, walls,
and the backs of nuns,
useful in their calling
for a country without
patience.

The lady teaches the aid the words,
repeating them, but she already has all
the words she needs.

Refocusing

Images of a lump, cancer, torsion — all
questions — flick blithely through
my brain. It should be scanned,
a little Doppler there might help. My ex-wife
would tell you it is.

The tech is respectful, does not
attempt to talk to me. Tells me what
he is doing, but does not converse.
The gel will be warm, and it is.
The wand manipulates me, pressure
making me move and wince.

I sort pictures
in my mind, a beautiful
girl I once knew. She is far away
from me now, though we are still
close. I would like to be holding her
hand. I would like to go home quiet
in the car. I would like to have her
tell me things will be alright.
She cannot.

There is too much
complication. Neither of us free. We are
older now, laden with responsibilities
we shoulder instead of avoiding, both of us
raised to do so.

We will find a way to be together, though
when and at what cost, we avoid mentioning.
These questions are not elephants, they are
the gun in the box at the top of the closet your
ten-year-old knows about.

Fear

You were the lost and found,
never claimed, that I took home.
Guilty, because you were never
mine.

And, one day,
the venetian bars of light that caress
the bed we share will turn
hard.

I know someone
will come calling, offer you
a home, never knowing they take
mine away.

Nietzsche
> *because sometimes your cat is the only one you can miss*

I watched you
for days tearing your hair
out and leaving it for me. Finally,
your thighs bald, you collapsed,
once again, on my chest.

Days later, I realized,
I had stopped smoking in the house,
Our nightly ritual of cigarettes and beer,
you on my chest, my smoke blown
softly over you,
what you were missing.

Three years later, you lay on the table.
The vet asking what you drank, my
cautious reply of tap water, her condescension
obvious. The fever ripping through you
with the end game drugs.

I apologized, weeping on the way home,
lighting a cigarette.

Exodus

I asked my hands to bleed, the last time,
last night. Tearing the roses out of the garden
and stacking them. The next owners can
wonder why, or simply turn them in
to the mulch pile.
        Displaced by our closed bedroom
door, sealed with blue flickering light
piercing the keyhole, I found work to do.
                                Darkness
under my fingernails — rotting leaves
placed, to help keep the moisture in, the heat, to help
Texas soil produce a spring tracery of red-veined
petals.
    Missing only the smell of jasmine, too newly
planted to produce. I left the jasmine, winter dormant,
and ready to take over the fence line. It will help obscure
the terror of the roses, as they brown. Help me forget
the immediacy I felt, alone,
                lingering in the car,
still. Pregnant with the smell of humus, dog,
and innocence. I feel the sandy mixture, closing over
with the roughness of scabs. Had I been a more attentive gardener,
calluses would have blocked the thorns.
                            Gently pulling
my hands from the plastic, leaving new blood
on the steering wheel. Tear-blurred rearview mirror filled
with morning, quickly left behind. Slight adjustments
allow me to see my son, old enough only to understand
the missing,
    asleep in the backseat.

## Reading

Under the blue sky, dog clouds chasing
balls of fluff, she reads
in the park.

States away, I watch them spin
on the carousel, her son's concern.
The speed is right, but mom
is far way, her foot lazy
as it draws in the dust.

What are you reading, mom?
*Beautiful words written by my friend.*
*Mom, don't cry, let's go play castle.*

She adjusts her crown, walks
to the jungle gym, the train
of her dress trailing text,
leaves slipping into the mote, before the bridge
is drawn tight.

Love is Religion

I have done everything my mother told me
not to do. I have built you up in my mind;
I have put you on a pedestal; I believe you
can do no wrong. I bend over backward
                            for you
as I can see no conflict, and I have
nothing to lose. I will worship at the feet
of love. I will kiss the silk hem of your
dress, and I will never regret
                            time we have
already spent. You could push me away
and break my heart. You could become
a raven, with the meat of me dangling
                            from
your talons. I believe in love. I believe the time
we've already had was worth giving you
the ability to destroy me. I believe all time
is borrowed, now.
                Any time that brings your
quiet smile is time I don't deserve and must
praise our god for providing. I am thankful
praise takes so many forms.

Poets

In reality, I think it is more
A mistake of breeding, and not
An achievement after which to strive.
Nor, in case someone were so strange,
Should you attempt to recreate in yourself
The lack of true interaction that creates
Us. We are an accident built out of lack
Of trust, and so, isolated and isolating.

Burn

A trash can I use for raku
blazes with poetry, desire,
I am inhaling the smoke of my past.
Need, men, women,
girls evaporate
into the ash of morning.

I prepare to be
in your embrace without
a past of failed caresses.
I cannot afford
these ghosts,
jeopardy among new fallen snow.

Notebooks

I will ask you who
you were thinking of when you
screamed your songs
in your bedroom,
a girl.

I'll ask. Though,
I shouldn't. And you,
you'll answer with boys
names other than mine,
of course. You will gauge
my reaction then
apologize.

Like Tolstoy,
I want to hand you my notebooks
Knowing full well they
will destroy
us.

Faith, Come Sunday

Do you truly believe the heat
Will die, and one of us will drift away
On gentle waves waking one day
Empty, as you imply, or maybe the strange
Desert we bore witness to in youth
Will consume us, steal the green heat we find
In the middle of the night,
That tears us from the strangle hold
Of sleep, because it is Sunday.
And, Sunday is always a day of mourning
A day of loss in which one of us
Is always leaving. The urge to faith,
I will not deny. But, we are two
Or more gathered together. We are
Our church, and I have never lost faith
Since rediscovering it.

I do not believe in a desert
Without oasis. Will you tell me
Of a day when you would rather I
Not rock you to sleep in my lap,
Our bodies lost together,
One in a darkness that recognizes
Only the two of us, blended?
A morning which ignores the pain
Of tearing us apart. That morning
will come when neither
Of us keeps the mourning and only the faith,
A faith demanding sacrifice no longer
And we spend our days exposed
To the sun, scarred, yet wrapped
In the balm of the green island's
Palm.

Pieces

I have felt the cold
tile of my heart
under my feet.
I understood reticence
and the desire to run
from me, not to me.
I am broken and you
want the pieces.

Will you collect me in your ashtray
like change or dangerous
screws found in parking lots you
trick yourself
into thinking you're saving from someone
else's tires?
Am I sparkling glass you cannot resist
touching?

I cannot explain the need to fit
into you,
and I will not resist the urge to bite
into perfect skin.
I never claimed to be safe,
quite the opposite.
I don't even want
my pieces.

Confession

— *for my son*

I am too afraid
now, to throw you high,
let you go — cannot trust the arc
of trajectory, cannot lose
contact.

Still, I try
to spin you, holding you tight
in my arms. Your laugh, not as wild or free,
but the speed sometimes defies the gravity
of loss.

You gave me that wild smile and laugh
seconds before pushing your teeth into your jaw,
falling against cold stone, the marble
vanity showing a shallow wound. I thought
you had swallowed the teeth.

Rushing you, naked from your bath,
to the changing table. You screaming separating
my tears from yours, sharing our hysteria.
I begged your forgiveness for turning my head,
for letting go.

Only at the ER, my shirt covered in blood,
you looking perfect in new PJs, the doctor asking
who needed to be looked at, did we find
the teeth, neatly embedded by the impact –
nestled against your adult teeth

hiding.

Left Hand of God

And, of course, I've been talking
to the wrong shoulder, asking how we
are going to Romeo and Juliet this shit
together. How the puzzle of distance and time
might finally be solved.

I'm angry and alone — abandoned.

I don't think either shoulder has an answer,
though one tells me to stay put
and the other says run.
I have loved you for years
and cannot reconcile myself
to the loss of every day

apart.

Laundry

There is something
strange about folding my son's clothes
when he is not here.
It is quiet mourning,
a remembrance, that allows
renewal.

I am forced to think
of all the times I've not
lived up to his smile. Allowed
his tears to fall before comforting
hurt feelings. Folding his pirate
blanket,

realizing he'll outgrow
it soon. I have one chance. Frightening
myself into immobility as I consider
his absence. A month in which I must
correct so much of my own
behavior.

He parts from me, taken
on father's day every year,
to spend solid time with his mother,
to waltz around a city full of whispers,
full of temptations, he *runs cars*, a game
he has made up.

He races barefoot
down the sidewalk as cars turn
onto Woodrow. I am left to worry
on broken glass and rusted nails,
on slippery perches atop washed SUVs,
on wet cheeks I cannot comfort.

It is this time, when I am still,
when I miss the broken silence he fills
with a voice of questions
and authoritative guesses. When
the silence is here,
so is the darkness.

Perfect Fit

If I really believed
that forever wasn't that long
or even had a notion of forever
I could have let go, trusted.
But, I do not believe that I will
ever ask and receive. I must take
and choose to be delivered of my
own hand. A terrible and perfect
burden. I am more than willing
to embrace, not suspend, a
belief in perfection now
over the burden of
belief in a then
a will be
a how.

Thirst

When you forget to blur
the lines,
When you cry yourself to sleep
from clarity,
When you are no longer fooling yourself
with the pillow in your arms and your tears
wet no shoulder,
You wake without kisses,
only the knowledge they are yours
and lost,
Tenderness is far away and she pays
as you do,
Then
Taste the bitter morning made all the more so
with birdsong you've laughed with
together.
Drink the sunlight that should catch her
hair, but glances off the sill, laden
with bottles.
Inhale the dust motes you treasured,
a visual for her scent, now heavy
with ash memory.
Touch your own skin, dormant, stagnant
without her fingertips.
Embrace the morning as you will
the earth.

## Creating Memory

I have been trying desperately
to digest your language, given me
in fits and bursts, sucking softly
on the pinks and reds, annoyed
with the tears your blue-lined worries
easily surface.

I am in love, but that is obvious
and a stupid thing to write. I am
swallowing each syllable after rolling
it like soy pearls over my tongue. I am
drunk on the structures of distance
and longing.

Tired, I reach out to you
at 3am, and you receive me in long
grasses and green leaf-topped hideaways.
Water cascades under our bed;
the sky never brightens; the stars
light exploring fingers.

If morning comes, the touch
of your lips on my eyelids will strip
the sleep away enough for us
to decide to spend the day
shuttered, alone, drifting
on dreams of new stars.

Homeless

I am flying away
from Cleveland, regret
heavy, seeking comfort
in my son's hand as we take off.
I tell him, once again, about time's
flow forward and expressing how
you feel, not to hide from heartbreak,
not to let fear rob you of possibility.
I am abstracting, but he knows
the reference.

It was Thanksgiving, and I was thankful
we were stealing kisses in our parent's cars.
My son playing with my childhood
Legos at his grandparent's as we shared each other
a few short miles away before parting
each night, like teenagers.
High on unrealized memories
and a future we can see clearly
together.

You are on another plane,
headed to your own state. Our trip
underlining sacrifice for what could have been
easy if we'd taken the chances we take now,
eyes steady over sad smiles, working
toward simple completion.

## Goodnight, Love

I have begun the falling
apart, the losing of you.
The gentle removal of your
perfections, the recognition of you
again as a memory. Once more,
the girl in the past, too good,
too pure, too talented
for me.

I got to touch you. I should
feel blessed. I saw you, received
the grace of your image. I kissed
your perfect lips, and I should
be satiated. Instead,
I am greedy.

And you have started
to remove your presence. I
understand. I will wait again, I
have before. I may come,
finally, to the realization
that you are an ideal,
you will not be attained. I can
give up, but not yet.

## Ash Morning

There is a wildfire burning,
consuming houses a few blocks away.
Smoke steals sleep, leaving residual
waking dreams.
         My fingers
trace the memory of your hip,
our bodies curled together.
I am trying to forget
the discoloration, the shift
in your eyes.
         Trees explode
as the water inside them boils
before you can see the flames
get close.
         I return
to your lavender scent,
the curl of your lip, your
hair in my car, forgotten
sunglasses and the Taos gallery
of tortured roses.
         It is coming,
consuming everything, destroying
balance, and there is no
rain.

## Tranquil

I don't care
that I've spent the last twenty-two
years trying to reclaim
the inability to say no. Trying
to get you to kiss me again
in the front seat of the car;
I don't even know whose
car it was.
You've asked.

It is the hollow I've found
after unchanged voices slip through
from an unwanted past.

It is the noise between the music
played too loud as I drink myself
to sleep that surrounds me.

It is the ghost of you lying
curled into me, my arms hugging
the morning's pillow.

It is the empty of the desert
that same morning promising a clear
ride into New Mexico mountains.

It is the thrum of the woman
who never leaves me between my legs
pulling me into headlight drunk altitude.

It is finding hope on the roadside
in a pile of rabbit, vomit, and anxiety
before seeing you again.

It is the tranquil of the overwrought.
And I thank you, under bruised sky,
for giving it back.

www.michaeltorok.com

www.ingramcontent.com/pod-product-compliance
Lightning Source LLC
Chambersburg PA
CBHW071741040426
42446CB00012B/2419